EMMANUEL JOSEPH

Leadership Mosaic, Bridging Cultural Differences for Global Business Excellence

Copyright © 2025 by Emmanuel Joseph

All rights reserved. No part of this publication may be reproduced, stored or transmitted in any form or by any means, electronic, mechanical, photocopying, recording, scanning, or otherwise without written permission from the publisher. It is illegal to copy this book, post it to a website, or distribute it by any other means without permission.

First edition

This book was professionally typeset on Reedsy.
Find out more at reedsy.com

Contents

1. Chapter 1: The Global Business Landscape — 1
2. Chapter 2: The Essence of Cultural Intelligence — 3
3. Chapter 3: The Role of Communication in Cross-Cultural... — 5
4. Chapter 4: Building Trust Across Cultures — 7
5. Chapter 5: Leveraging Cultural Diversity for Innovation — 8
6. Chapter 6: Ethical Leadership in a Global Context — 10
7. Chapter 7: Navigating Cross-Cultural Negotiations — 12
8. Chapter 8: Leading Global Teams — 14
9. Chapter 9: Cross-Cultural Conflict Resolution — 16
10. Chapter 10: Cultural Adaptation and Flexibility — 18
11. Chapter 11: The Power of Cross-Cultural Collaboration — 20
12. Chapter 12: Leadership Styles Across Cultures — 22
13. Chapter 13: The Role of Technology in Cross-Cultural... — 24
14. Chapter 14: Measuring Success in Cross-Cultural Leadership — 26
15. Chapter 15: The Future of Cross-Cultural Leadership — 28

1

Chapter 1: The Global Business Landscape

In today's interconnected world, businesses no longer operate within the confines of their home countries. Globalization has opened up new markets, opportunities, and challenges. Companies must navigate diverse cultures, languages, and business practices to succeed internationally. This chapter explores the importance of cultural awareness in global business and how it impacts leadership strategies.

The rise of multinational corporations has transformed the business landscape, making cross-cultural competence a critical skill for leaders. Understanding cultural nuances can make or break business deals and partnerships. Leaders must develop the ability to communicate effectively, build trust, and foster collaboration across cultural boundaries.

Effective leadership in a global context requires an appreciation of different cultural values, beliefs, and behaviors. Leaders must be adaptable and open-minded, willing to learn from diverse perspectives. This chapter delves into the key cultural dimensions that influence business interactions and decision-making.

As businesses expand internationally, leaders must navigate complex cultural dynamics to achieve success. This chapter highlights the role of cultural intelligence in global leadership, emphasizing the need for continuous learning and self-awareness. By embracing cultural differences, leaders can drive innovation, foster inclusivity, and achieve sustainable growth.

2

Chapter 2: The Essence of Cultural Intelligence

Cultural intelligence (CQ) is the ability to understand and adapt to different cultural contexts. It is a crucial skill for leaders in the global business environment. This chapter explores the components of cultural intelligence and its significance in leadership.

Cultural intelligence comprises four key elements: cognitive, motivational, behavioral, and metacognitive. Cognitive CQ involves understanding cultural norms and values, while motivational CQ reflects the leader's interest and confidence in interacting with different cultures. Behavioral CQ refers to the ability to adjust one's behavior in response to cultural differences, and metacognitive CQ involves self-awareness and reflection on cultural interactions.

Leaders with high cultural intelligence can navigate complex cultural situations with ease. They are adept at building relationships, managing conflicts, and leading diverse teams. This chapter provides practical strategies for developing and enhancing cultural intelligence, including cultural immersion, training programs, and reflective practices.

In the global business landscape, cultural intelligence is a competitive advantage. Leaders who can bridge cultural gaps are more likely to succeed in international markets. This chapter emphasizes the importance of continuous learning and development in cultivating cultural intelligence. By fostering an inclusive and culturally aware leadership style, leaders can drive organizational success and global business excellence.

3

Chapter 3: The Role of Communication in Cross-Cultural Leadership

Effective communication is the cornerstone of successful cross-cultural leadership. This chapter explores the challenges and opportunities of communication in a global business context. It highlights the importance of understanding cultural communication styles and adapting one's approach to different cultural norms.

Communication styles vary widely across cultures, from direct and explicit to indirect and nuanced. Leaders must be aware of these differences and adjust their communication strategies accordingly. This chapter provides insights into the impact of language, nonverbal cues, and context on cross-cultural communication. It also discusses the role of active listening and empathy in building rapport and trust.

Miscommunication can lead to misunderstandings, conflicts, and lost business opportunities. Leaders must develop the skills to bridge communication gaps and create an environment of open and transparent dialogue. This chapter offers practical tips for improving cross-cultural communication, including language training, cultural mediation, and the use of technology.

In the global business arena, effective communication is a key driver of success. Leaders who can communicate clearly and confidently across cultures can foster collaboration, innovation, and business growth. This chapter underscores the importance of communication skills in cross-cultural leadership and provides tools and techniques for enhancing these skills.

4

Chapter 4: Building Trust Across Cultures

Trust is the foundation of any successful business relationship. In a global context, building trust across cultures can be challenging. This chapter explores the dynamics of trust in cross-cultural interactions and offers strategies for establishing and maintaining trust in global business settings.

Cultural differences can impact perceptions of trustworthiness and credibility. Leaders must understand these differences and take steps to build trust with diverse stakeholders. This chapter discusses the role of cultural values, such as individualism and collectivism, in shaping trust. It also examines the impact of historical relationships and societal norms on trust-building.

Building trust across cultures requires intentional effort and cultural sensitivity. Leaders must demonstrate integrity, competence, and empathy. This chapter provides practical guidance on how to build trust through consistent communication, transparency, and cultural competence. It also highlights the importance of managing expectations and delivering on promises.

In the global business environment, trust is a critical enabler of collaboration and success. Leaders who can build and sustain trust across cultures can create a competitive advantage for their organizations. This chapter emphasizes the importance of trust in cross-cultural leadership and offers strategies for cultivating trust in diverse business contexts.

5

Chapter 5: Leveraging Cultural Diversity for Innovation

Cultural diversity is a powerful driver of innovation and creativity. This chapter explores how leaders can harness the potential of diverse teams to drive business excellence. It discusses the benefits of cultural diversity and provides strategies for fostering an inclusive and innovative organizational culture.

Diverse teams bring a wealth of perspectives, experiences, and ideas. Leaders must create an environment where these differences are valued and leveraged for innovation. This chapter highlights the role of inclusive leadership in fostering a culture of creativity and collaboration. It also discusses the challenges of managing diverse teams and offers solutions for overcoming these challenges.

Inclusive leadership involves recognizing and addressing biases, promoting diversity and inclusion, and creating opportunities for all team members to contribute. This chapter provides practical tips for building diverse and inclusive teams, including recruitment strategies, mentorship programs, and cultural competence training.

Innovation thrives in a diverse and inclusive environment. Leaders who embrace cultural diversity can drive business growth and competitiveness. This chapter underscores the importance of leveraging cultural diversity for

CHAPTER 5: LEVERAGING CULTURAL DIVERSITY FOR INNOVATION

innovation and provides actionable insights for fostering an inclusive and innovative organizational culture.

6

Chapter 6: Ethical Leadership in a Global Context

Ethical leadership is crucial for building a sustainable and responsible business. This chapter explores the principles of ethical leadership and their application in a global context. It discusses the challenges of navigating ethical dilemmas across cultures and offers strategies for maintaining ethical integrity.

Cultural differences can impact perceptions of ethical behavior. Leaders must understand these differences and navigate complex ethical dilemmas with cultural sensitivity. This chapter provides insights into the role of cultural values, such as power distance and uncertainty avoidance, in shaping ethical behavior. It also discusses the importance of ethical leadership in building trust and reputation.

Ethical leadership involves making decisions that are aligned with the organization's values and principles. Leaders must demonstrate accountability, transparency, and social responsibility. This chapter offers practical guidance on how to uphold ethical standards in a global context, including the development of ethical policies, training programs, and stakeholder engagement.

In the global business environment, ethical leadership is a key driver of long-term success. Leaders who prioritize ethical behavior can build a strong reputation, foster stakeholder trust, and create a positive impact on society. This chapter emphasizes the importance of ethical leadership in cross-cultural contexts and provides strategies for maintaining ethical integrity.

7

Chapter 7: Navigating Cross-Cultural Negotiations

Negotiation is a critical skill for leaders in the global business environment. This chapter explores the dynamics of cross-cultural negotiations and provides strategies for achieving successful outcomes. It discusses the impact of cultural differences on negotiation styles and offers practical tips for navigating complex negotiations.

Cultural differences can influence negotiation behaviors, such as communication styles, decision-making processes, and conflict resolution strategies. Leaders must understand these differences and adapt their negotiation approach accordingly. This chapter provides insights into the role of cultural dimensions, such as individualism vs. collectivism and high-context vs. low-context communication, in shaping negotiation behaviors.

Effective negotiation requires preparation, cultural awareness, and flexibility. This chapter offers practical guidance on how to conduct cross-cultural negotiations, including building relationships, managing conflicts, and finding common ground. It also discusses the importance of cultural intelligence in achieving successful negotiation outcomes.

In the global business arena, successful negotiation is a key driver of business growth and competitiveness. Leaders who can navigate cross-

CHAPTER 7: NAVIGATING CROSS-CULTURAL NEGOTIATIONS

cultural negotiations can build strong partnerships, resolve conflicts, and achieve strategic objectives. This chapter emphasizes the importance of cross-cultural negotiation skills and provides actionable insights for enhancing these skills.

8

Chapter 8: Leading Global Teams

Leading global teams presents unique challenges and opportunities. This chapter explores the dynamics of global team leadership and provides strategies for managing diverse and dispersed teams. It discusses the importance of cultural competence, communication, and collaboration in leading global teams.

Global teams are often diverse in terms of cultural backgrounds, languages, and work styles. Leaders must create an environment where these differences are valued and leveraged for team success. This chapter provides insights into the role of inclusive leadership in fostering collaboration and cohesion in global teams. It also discusses the challenges of managing virtual teams and offers solutions for overcoming these challenges.

Effective global team leadership involves building trust, facilitating communication, and promoting a shared vision. This chapter offers practical tips for leading global teams, including team-building activities, cultural competence training, and technology tools. It also highlights the importance of continuous learning and development in enhancing global team leadership skills.

In the global business environment, leading successful global teams is a critical capability for leaders. Leaders who can navigate the complexities of global team dynamics can drive innovation, collaboration, and business excellence. This chapter emphasizes the importance of global team leadership and provides actionable insights for enhancing these skills.

9

Chapter 9: Cross-Cultural Conflict Resolution

Conflict is an inevitable part of business interactions, especially in a global context. This chapter explores the dynamics of cross-cultural conflict and provides strategies for resolving conflicts effectively. It discusses the impact of cultural differences on conflict behaviors and offers practical tips for managing conflicts across cultures.

Cultural differences can influence how conflicts are perceived and addressed. Leaders must understand these differences and develop the skills to manage cross-cultural conflicts effectively. This chapter provides insights into the role of cultural dimensions, such as power distance and individualism vs. collectivism, in shaping conflict behaviors. It also discusses the importance of cultural intelligence in resolving conflicts.

Effective conflict resolution requires active listening, empathy, and cultural sensitivity. Leaders must develop the skills to identify and address the root causes of conflicts, rather than just the symptoms. This chapter provides practical strategies for managing cross-cultural conflicts, including mediation, negotiation, and cultural competence training.

In a global business environment, conflicts can arise from misunderstandings, miscommunications, and differing cultural values. Leaders must be proactive in preventing and addressing conflicts to maintain a positive and productive work environment. This chapter discusses the importance of creating a culture of open dialogue and mutual respect to minimize conflicts.

Successful conflict resolution can strengthen relationships and enhance team cohesion. Leaders who can navigate cross-cultural conflicts effectively can build trust, foster collaboration, and drive business success. This chapter emphasizes the importance of conflict resolution skills in cross-cultural leadership and provides actionable insights for enhancing these skills.

10

Chapter 10: Cultural Adaptation and Flexibility

Cultural adaptation and flexibility are essential for leaders in the global business environment. This chapter explores the importance of adapting to different cultural contexts and provides strategies for developing cultural flexibility. It discusses the challenges of cultural adaptation and offers practical tips for overcoming these challenges.

Cultural adaptation involves adjusting one's behavior, communication style, and decision-making processes to align with different cultural norms and expectations. Leaders must be open-minded and willing to learn from diverse perspectives. This chapter provides insights into the role of cultural intelligence in cultural adaptation and offers strategies for enhancing cultural flexibility.

Flexibility is a key attribute of successful global leaders. Leaders who can adapt to different cultural contexts can build strong relationships, navigate complex situations, and drive business success. This chapter offers practical guidance on how to develop cultural flexibility, including cultural immersion, mentorship, and continuous learning.

In the global business environment, cultural adaptation and flexibility are critical for achieving business excellence. Leaders who can navigate cultural differences with ease can create a competitive advantage for their

CHAPTER 10: CULTURAL ADAPTATION AND FLEXIBILITY

organizations. This chapter emphasizes the importance of cultural adaptation and flexibility in cross-cultural leadership and provides actionable insights for enhancing these skills.

11

Chapter 11: The Power of Cross-Cultural Collaboration

Cross-cultural collaboration is a powerful driver of business innovation and growth. This chapter explores the dynamics of cross-cultural collaboration and provides strategies for fostering effective collaboration across cultures. It discusses the benefits of cross-cultural collaboration and offers practical tips for overcoming collaboration challenges.

Diverse teams bring unique perspectives, experiences, and ideas that can drive innovation and creativity. Leaders must create an environment where cross-cultural collaboration is encouraged and valued. This chapter provides insights into the role of inclusive leadership in fostering collaboration and offers strategies for building collaborative teams.

Effective cross-cultural collaboration requires clear communication, mutual respect, and shared goals. Leaders must develop the skills to facilitate collaboration and manage conflicts. This chapter offers practical guidance on how to enhance cross-cultural collaboration, including team-building activities, cultural competence training, and technology tools.

In the global business environment, cross-cultural collaboration is a key driver of business success. Leaders who can foster collaboration across cultures can drive innovation, enhance team performance, and achieve

CHAPTER 11: THE POWER OF CROSS-CULTURAL COLLABORATION

strategic objectives. This chapter emphasizes the importance of cross-cultural collaboration and provides actionable insights for enhancing these skills.

12

Chapter 12: Leadership Styles Across Cultures

Leadership styles vary widely across cultures, influenced by cultural values, beliefs, and practices. This chapter explores different leadership styles and their impact on global business. It discusses the importance of understanding and adapting to different leadership styles in cross-cultural contexts.

Cultural dimensions, such as power distance, individualism vs. collectivism, and uncertainty avoidance, shape leadership behaviors and expectations. Leaders must be aware of these cultural dimensions and adjust their leadership style accordingly. This chapter provides insights into the role of cultural intelligence in adapting leadership styles and offers practical tips for enhancing leadership effectiveness.

Effective global leaders are adaptable and culturally aware. They can navigate different cultural contexts with ease and build strong relationships with diverse stakeholders. This chapter offers practical guidance on how to develop and adapt leadership styles for different cultural contexts, including cultural competence training, mentorship, and continuous learning.

In the global business environment, understanding and adapting to different leadership styles is critical for achieving business excellence. Leaders who can navigate cultural differences in leadership can create a competitive advantage for their organizations. This chapter emphasizes the importance of cultural intelligence in leadership and provides actionable insights for enhancing leadership effectiveness.

13

Chapter 13: The Role of Technology in Cross-Cultural Leadership

Technology plays a crucial role in facilitating cross-cultural leadership and collaboration. This chapter explores the impact of technology on global business and provides strategies for leveraging technology to enhance cross-cultural leadership. It discusses the benefits and challenges of using technology in cross-cultural contexts.

Technology can bridge geographical and cultural gaps, enabling leaders to communicate and collaborate effectively across borders. This chapter provides insights into the role of technology in facilitating cross-cultural communication, collaboration, and decision-making. It also discusses the importance of digital literacy and cultural competence in leveraging technology.

Effective use of technology requires a balance between digital tools and human interaction. Leaders must develop the skills to use technology effectively while maintaining cultural sensitivity. This chapter offers practical guidance on how to leverage technology for cross-cultural leadership, including virtual communication tools, collaboration platforms, and cultural competence training.

In the global business environment, technology is a powerful enabler of cross-cultural leadership. Leaders who can leverage technology effectively can enhance communication, collaboration, and business performance. This chapter emphasizes the importance of digital literacy and cultural competence in leveraging technology for cross-cultural leadership and provides actionable insights for enhancing these skills.

14

Chapter 14: Measuring Success in Cross-Cultural Leadership

Measuring success in cross-cultural leadership requires a comprehensive approach that considers both quantitative and qualitative factors. This chapter explores the metrics and indicators for assessing cross-cultural leadership effectiveness. It discusses the importance of continuous improvement and feedback in achieving global business excellence.

Quantitative metrics, such as financial performance, market share, and employee productivity, provide a clear measure of business success. However, qualitative factors, such as employee engagement, cultural competence, and stakeholder satisfaction, are equally important in assessing cross-cultural leadership effectiveness. This chapter provides insights into the role of cultural intelligence in measuring success and offers practical tips for developing comprehensive assessment frameworks.

Continuous improvement and feedback are critical for enhancing cross-cultural leadership skills. Leaders must be open to feedback, willing to learn from their experiences, and committed to ongoing development. This chapter offers practical guidance on how to create a culture of continuous improvement, including feedback mechanisms, mentorship programs, and cultural competence training.

CHAPTER 14: MEASURING SUCCESS IN CROSS-CULTURAL LEADERSHIP

In the global business environment, measuring success in cross-cultural leadership is essential for achieving business excellence. Leaders who can assess their effectiveness and make continuous improvements can drive innovation, enhance team performance, and achieve strategic objectives. This chapter emphasizes the importance of comprehensive assessment and continuous improvement in cross-cultural leadership and provides actionable insights for enhancing these skills.

15

Chapter 15: The Future of Cross-Cultural Leadership

The future of cross-cultural leadership is shaped by global trends and emerging challenges. This chapter explores the future of cross-cultural leadership and provides strategies for preparing for the evolving global business landscape. It discusses the impact of technological advancements, demographic shifts, and geopolitical changes on cross-cultural leadership.

Technological advancements, such as artificial intelligence, automation, and digital transformation, are reshaping the global business environment. Leaders must develop the skills to navigate these changes and leverage technology for cross-cultural leadership. This chapter provides insights into the role of digital literacy and cultural competence in preparing for the future of cross-cultural leadership.

Demographic shifts, such as the rise of the millennial workforce and increasing diversity, are changing the dynamics of cross-cultural leadership. Leaders must create inclusive and adaptive organizational cultures to attract and retain top talent. This chapter offers practical guidance on how to build inclusive and adaptive organizations, including diversity and inclusion initiatives, mentorship programs, and cultural competence training.

Geopolitical changes, such as trade wars, regulatory changes, and political

CHAPTER 15: THE FUTURE OF CROSS-CULTURAL LEADERSHIP

instability, pose challenges for cross-cultural leadership. Leaders must develop the skills to navigate these challenges and build resilient organizations. This chapter emphasizes the importance of strategic thinking, cultural intelligence, and adaptability in preparing for the future of cross-cultural leadership.

In the global business environment, the future of cross-cultural leadership is shaped by global trends and emerging challenges. Leaders who can prepare for these changes and develop the skills to navigate the evolving landscape can create a competitive advantage for their organizations. This chapter highlights the importance of continuous learning, cultural competence, and strategic thinking in preparing for the future of cross-cultural leadership and provides actionable insights for enhancing these skills.

Description:

In an era where global boundaries blur and international markets burgeon, effective leadership transcends the mere management of an organization. "Leadership Mosaic: Bridging Cultural Differences for Global Business Excellence" delves deep into the heart of what it takes to lead in a diverse world. This book is a rich tapestry, weaving together the critical aspects of cultural intelligence, effective communication, ethical leadership, and innovation, all aimed at achieving excellence in the global business landscape.

This comprehensive guide is divided into 15 meticulously crafted chapters, each exploring a unique facet of cross-cultural leadership. From understanding the global business landscape to building trust across cultures, from leveraging diversity for innovation to navigating complex cross-cultural negotiations, the book offers a robust framework for leaders seeking to excel on the international stage. It provides insightful strategies, practical tips, and reflective practices to help leaders develop the cultural competence necessary for success.

Readers will discover the essence of cultural intelligence, the importance of effective communication, and the power of trust and collaboration. They will learn how to lead diverse global teams, resolve cross-cultural conflicts, and adapt leadership styles to different cultural contexts. The book also highlights the ethical considerations in a global setting and the role of technology in facilitating cross-cultural leadership.

"Leadership Mosaic" is not just a guide; it's an invitation to embrace cultural diversity and turn it into a strategic advantage. It is a must-read for aspiring leaders, business professionals, and anyone interested in understanding the complexities and opportunities of global business leadership. Through its engaging and well-researched content, this book equips readers with the knowledge and tools to navigate the dynamic and ever-evolving global business environment, ultimately driving business excellence and fostering a culture of inclusivity and innovation.

www.ingramcontent.com/pod-product-compliance
Lightning Source LLC
LaVergne TN
LVHW020502080526
838202LV00057B/6106